Critical acclair

"Highly recommended."
- *Canadian Materials Magazine*

"Wing paints a provocative portrait of comic life..."
- *Globe & Mail*

"John Wing's poetry brims with the fullness of everyday life. And like life itself, it is filled with ironies and complexities. On the surface, everything seems so simple and clear, but far beneath his words is a radiance and wisdom, you can't help but turn to embrace this, like the earth spinning around to face the sun."
- Marty Gervais, *The Windsor Star*

"There are poems in this collection that are as deeply moving when the culminating syllables reach you as anything new you'll read this year. *Moscow Nights* has a last line that's so good the rest of the poem can hardly wait for you to get there. They do wait, though, these poems, and the lines do arrive, and the timing of the whole business often feels exactly right, it's the way art's supposed to feel but not nearly often enough does. I'm talking about *good* art, you understand."
- Don Coles, *Governor General's Award Winner*

"John Wing Jr. takes us down the path of foiling the crowd. He taunts and teases and plays with every line delivered. With every story told and situation felt I cannot but condone the poetry as an invitation into the palatial charm that is human nature.
    He writes with authority and conviction. His work is controlled and outrageous. The beauty and the stringent reaching for notes out of range and rolling words into ideals. For as Mr. John Wing Jr. puts it in *Chief*:
    "Death questions the living."
- T. Anders Carson, *The Danforth Review*

To David,

EXCUSES

[signature]

APRIL - 2006

EXCUSES

POEMS

BY

JOHN WING JR.

mosaic press

Library and Archives Canada Cataloguing in Publication

Wing, John, 1959-
    Excuses / John Wing.

Poems.
ISBN 0-88962-852-1

    I. Title.

PS8595.I5953E93 2005   C811'.54   C2005-906002-6

Publishing by Mosaic Press, offices and warehouse at 1252 Speers
Rd., units 1 & 2, Oakville, On L6L 5N9, Canada and Mosaic
Press, PMB 145, 4500 Witmer Industrial Estates, Niagara Falls,
NY, 14305-1386, U.S.A.

Copyright © John Wing Jr., 2005
ISBN 0-88962-852-1
cover photo by haster
Design by Josh Goskey

Mosaic Press in Canada:
1252 Speers Road, Units 1 & 2,
Oakville, Ontario
L6L 5N9
Phone/Fax: 905-825-2130
info@mosaic-press.com

Mosaic Press in U.S.A.:
4500 Witmer Industrial Estates
PMB 145, Niagara Falls, NY
14305-1386
Phone/Fax: 1-800-387-8992
info@mosaic-press.com

www.mosaic-press.com

Nothing is funnier than unhappiness.

Samuel Beckett

*Now a man can spend a lot of time
wondering what was on Jack Ruby's mind.*

Billy Bragg

TABLE OF CONTENTS

For Rachel and Isabel

MORTGAGES

As apparitional as sails that cross
Some page of figures to be filed away;
-- Till elevators drop us from our day...

Hart Crane

Mortgages

This is what I own,
along with this
new house in California.

I own fault. I own blame.
Some spindled child
whose eyes remain hopeful
that what he knows is true
will not be true today.
I own fear. Shame.

I own insult. The thousand injuries
of Fortunato, the thanking of Jesus
for the memory of all that is owed me.
I own Poe, and his vision, chained
up, bricked in.

I own wood that must be scraped
and painted, lead dust, radon,
fear of death, trees I pay others
to cut down. I own mistakes, thefts,
and a strange dormant virus
that makes everyone wonder.

I own a small town I cannot leave
and will never return to. I own
cemetery photographs, proof
of stone. I own the sound
history makes when repeating itself.

More than nine years have passed
since the last big quake here. Even
the books I own have forgotten.

30 June – 1 July 2003
Sunland Ca.

Moscow Nights

She says
You have never read the Russians,
So how could you understand me?

So I plow through Pasternak,
wondering if she is Lara, lost
on the train to Siberia.

I destroy Dostoievsky,
and she is the idiot murderess,
the degenerate gambler,
with all these brothers.

I translate Tolstoy,
pummel Pushkin, groan
over Gorky and Gogol,
dead souls.

I hide these square piles
of grand scope sadness under
our bed, afraid she will think
I'm trying too hard.

That was nice, she murmurs after.
I almost came. Is that better
than actual climax, I ask?
She sighs her deep, winter palace sigh.

Spring 2002

Archaeology

When they find the casinos,
the piles of silvercoppers in the sifted
earth, the underground lapdance
chambers of the kings, will the scientists
discuss heathen rituals, decipher
the lost Slotmachine language, or just
leave skull-size theories lying around?

After the fourth ice age, the formica
ark will strike the reef that becomes
a mountain, every species disembarking
in a neat line to thank the screen-gods
for deliverance, seeing the great rivers
begin to form again, along
the fallout-colored horizon.

When they find the black tablets
packed with yellow names, some will
scoff at the hideous notion that they
might have evolved from some lame,
opposable-thumb group, while others
will simply stare for hours at three cherries,
knowing there is within a secret, a key.

August 2002 – February 2003

Yes, I'll Hold

No one said it would be
a cakewalk, a bag of shells
or a bowl of cherries, which
I don't even like. Even the beer
commercials that call their product
'easy drinking', as though millions
of people have great difficulty
drinking beer, have disclaimers
in case hard drinkers, who also dislike
cherries, find their endings
at the speed of glass.

A wino stopped me in the street once
and said, 'Think of this; if at first you
don't succeed, whose fault was it?'

No one said marriage is like a bad bank.
Eventually you lose interest. My father
tried to tell me a great many things, but
so many of them came true I stopped
listening. When my parents are gone,
all I'll have are the things they told me.

No one mentioned that while success
has many pitfalls, failure is a smooth
and untaxed road. I had to find
that one out myself. Or if you're
a whole day late, it doesn't really matter
if you're a dollar short. Count on it.

No one said the horseshit gets so high
you don't even notice the smell anymore.
They said, 'Wear a hat in case it rains.'
And if it didn't rain, and you were
the only one on the field in a goddamn
rain hat, it became a story to tell your
psychiatrist or your grandchild, or
the first scene, the pivotal scene,
in the novel you'll never write.

No one told me anything
while I was listening.

5 April, 2002
Dutch Antilles

The Great Hockey Player

The great hockey player, now retired,
signed autographs at the small table
by the door. He seemed tiny, with his
nice teeth and factory-tested hair, but he
still had those bulging slapshot muscles.

He had photographs for sale.
Color glossies from the bygone.
Fifty goals almost commonplace now.
Helmets make it hard to imagine.
Young eyes widened at bareheaded goalies.

The fathers told their sons what was what,
using modern stars' names to make them
understand what the great hockey player meant
to us. He signed his name with a flourish
each time, smiling and accepting cash.

Later, he got up on stage and told
dirty jokes, and everyone laughed hard,
nudging each other in disbelief. The great
hockey player, eh? Odd, the things that make
you grateful you have daughters.

February 2003 – January 2004
Sarnia, Ontario – Sunland, California

Now

The non-compliant sun
drives out the black bikinis
and pink-beige skin.

Some pass so near, casting
shadows on my pen. I notice
everything now.

Reflection makes the true, the wished-
for past, alive. Fantasy's long arm,
the new-car smell of nostalgia.

Now the hospital is my dreams.
I awake knowing someone
will come for my blood.

The blue rubber tube knots
on my arm, the red vials
clink on the bedsheet.

Still alive, although now
I've been out there. But I
stood it off. Stiff-armed it.

They packed me in ice
one night. My first real inkling
of a not-original idea.

The doctor strolls in, the one
whose name I love to pronounce,
razorwire notebook in hand.

She has a camera this time, too,
to snap my ravages for a generation
of students. I am awake with

arrow speed. In the bathroom
light, I check the fading spots,
perfect reminders.

I recall people who have
walked by, casting their long
shadows on me.

A girl comes into view. All right,
a woman, shining her welcome
upon me, beaded, strange.

A tarot reader, in the square
in New Orleans on that perfect
shellfish summer day, who said,

'You will have major health problems
after you turn forty.'   *Crazy bitch.*
'But you will recover.' *Oh. Okay.*

5 July, 2002
Grand Cayman

Career Day

Career day at my daughter's school,
moms and dads corralled outside, then
herded in by the assistant. Everybody's
here: fireman, cop, accountant, engineer,
pastor...(Pastor? Oh, Lutheran. Okay)
lawyer, radiologist, reporter, garbageman.
(I'm next to him) Names are called, and one
by one they come up and stand by their parent,
telling the class what that parent does.

I'm last, and when Isabel's name is finally
called, she scrambles up, loving every spot-lit
moment, and says, "This is my Daddy. He makes
people laugh." "No, dear," says the teacher. "What
does he do for a living?" "He makes people laugh,"
Isabel insists in her perfect, five-year-old way.
"Oh," says the teacher, getting it. "Your father is
a comedian." Isabel nods vigourously. I shrug,
and everyone looks at me funny.

26 Sept. 2004
Caribbean Sea

Moby Dick

I disembark at Pier 90, 50th and 12th.
A rainchill Sunday, me without a coat
or sweater – who cares? I have several
hours to walk around New York.

Haven't been here since September, 2001,
two days before the towers fell and
nothing changed but the skyline.
And the fear. But this morning holds

no fear as I walk to 42nd and 5th.
Across from the public library, so large
it might take years to find a book,
I buy cigars. It takes two hours

to get eight streets up and seven
avenues over. This is the city
of the window pause, the searching
eye. Like Moby Dick, each venture

into its endlessness reveals new treasures.
Brick and brownstone, newsstand and street
hawker, the horse-clop of the walkers,
all intent on their destinies. No more

porno store clusters in Times Square.
Too bad. I don't have time to search
out their new locations. But I have
all the other time. Slip-zagging

along Broadway, I see Roseland,
an ancient ballroom dance hall.
Later, a fated glance finds the Brill building,
where the songwriters wrote all the hits.

There is a perfect loneliness here, the feeling
of all that is larger awaiting. The sizzle-smell
of hot meat, steam into smoke, howl of buses
and buskers, harpies and harpooneers.

Melville wrote, 'Better to sleep with a sober cannibal
than a drunken Christian'. It is a drizzled Sunday
and everyone is not in church, but like me,
wandering through the waves.

Oct 20 – 31
New York – Bermuda – Reno – Los Angeles

Shuttle Bus

A five-lane-thick line of cars
red-lights the road. The signs are green
with only white names and numbers,
like gravestones. The last pale
of blue day fades behind us.
The sky falls like ink.

Two people sitting in front of me
are in love. Or, at least, she is.
She stares at him in that everything-
will-be-all-right way, while she wonders
how good a husband he'll make. Will he
rent the movies she likes? Make sure
she is satisfied before he finishes?
Understand everything she'll never
say, never tell?

The traffic thickens and we move
like porridge. Maybe she's not in love.
Maybe I am.

7 February, 2003
Los Angeles

14 • *Excuses*

Waiting For a Bus in Alberta

A woman carrying
most of what she owns
stops to go through
the pebbled ashtray,
choosing dead cigarettes
for reanimation.

Some days, my career
is a dead cigarette.
The money dries up
like an ancient wash,
the red dust
weeping for rain.

But I remain,
chained to ownership,
waiting for buses,
adding up future
dental bills
and school fees

I have lost
the seasons,
the ability to sustain
myself against the cold.
the thread, the urge
to conquer.

A model-thin
blonde strides by,
a cross tattooed
on her navel.
God help me, I would
be crucified there.

Summer 2004

DRAFTS

And up the paths
The endless altered people came,
Washing at their identity.

Philip Larkin

Drafts

A crooked jacket never stops me.
When I hug myself, only
my head is visible.

If I am honest
I am not honest.

Someone in my hotel room once
told me, in street-lit darkness,
how he killed a man, a rapist.

It was a long story, and all I could
think was, whether it was true or not,
it didn't impress me.

The plausible (myth) so easily
becomes the legend (lie).

Last night, the telephone solicitor
asked me how I was, and when I told her,
I could tell she didn't really care.

The woman I sleep with
never tells me anything.

I caught a fish once. A big rainbow.
Threw it back and never told anyone,
even the murderer in the next bed.

I have rewritten
everything.

18 February 2002
Antigua

Decisions

My mind is made up,
like a story you tell a customs official,
like the incredible excuse that hides the real reason,
like your bed when company comes over,
like a whore.

I've made up my mind,
covered the spots, put on the base,
lined the mind's eye black,
filled out the brows, highlighted
the intellectual cheekbones and clipped
the offending nostril hairs, drawing blood.

My mind and I have made up,
cleaned the slate, painted over
the graffiti. No more seven-way
conversations with voice-fractions
in the idiotic idioms. No more self-hating
operas bolstered with statistics over
the learned-by-rote math grid.

My mind is made up,
like a tale everyone tells differently,
like an acid-riff about listening to trees,
like the same answer to all questions.
My mind is made up tonight
and ready to go, dressed as
a figment of my imagination.

15 August 2002
Sunland, Ca.

Killings

The silent barbed-wire fence
holds the shredded remains
of a crucified owl.

The car goes by it so fast,
the image can only be reconstructed
years elsewhere.

Never touch a dead bird.
Even the one you thrillingly
murdered with a lucky stone.

Under the ice, the pure lime-water
shows a circle of golden perch
taking shots, in turn, at a dangling minnow.

The 300-grain steeljacket reaches
the elk before the sound of the gun.
He falls as though he was trained to die this way.

The unfeathered baby sparrow fell
out of the nest. I killed it.
Nothing else to do.

Strangling a small dog is easy.
Look for the claw scars on the wrist
of the driver as the fences rush by.

November – December 2002

Palm Springs

How far will you live?
How long will you lie?
Speaking of this again
and again.

The grass is brown here,
the sun blue. Everyone
speaks in tongues. The soul
is reversed, like a jacket
prized in adolescence.

The two sides look ridiculous
until you see the water
running through the concrete
and begin to doubt God,
feeling a smile deep
in your stomach.

Nothing breeds
in the deep rock. Everything
flows down. You feel
the cold in your throat,
the air in your toes.

17 April 2003   Palm Springs, Ca.

This is Only the Beginning

link-metal brain undercarriage

to the last man

calling all cars
calling all cars

Operation Enduring Bullshit
is underway

fan the humid generation
push the envelope
scorn the margins
resist the lines
leave the syllables –

don't read this
burn this

this poem will self-destruct
in – wait
don't shout
stop shouting

the horse whores are coming

log the infinite echo's time

Autumn 2002

Bryde's Whale

The fish are leaving now.
Three hundred right whales left,
they say. Though how they know
for sure escapes me. Some days
everything escapes me. Poems fly
off as I read the paper. Your cup of coffee
strong and un-sugared , escapes me
as we pass sections across
a blind table.

The giant harpoon gun signaled
the real end. No more brave men
rowing to the cadence-call, no more
Queequegs on the transom. Just fire-one,
direct hit, reverse it, keening whine
as the line backs in, crane it up from
the blood-soaked waves, and the cutters
do the rest, time and again. Bones
for dresses, lamp oil, sticky boots and steam.

Love is a factory ship, a store full
of rigid toys. A job. We are hungry
and we eat. When it's gone, we exhaust
a new flavour. Bryde's whale, whale shark,
giant ray. The light stream heats
your eyelids until they open like oysters.
The movement takes me from lesion-dreams,
empty gum-scapes, into wondering
if today will be more than our usual
search for meat and birdsong?

Somewhere there are old men,
whose brains remain image-bright .
Square-mile pods and seal rivers.
An endless flow of food and tool, the perfect taste
blood-whipped into frenzy.
But the fish are leaving now. Escaping
into books, distorted into legend,
silent as grey water.

5 Aug, 2003
Sunland, Ca.

Wild Bill

Was it really five men
all at once? Really?

During the buffalo days,
piling hump-skins on a mule wagon,
trading for bread and flesh
at the post, winning a saloon hand
too many, rising to slay any accuser
fool enough to lay a finger on his iron,
following the herd until the herd was gone.
And the word spread, as word tends to do.

First came the idiots. The plastered furiosi,
young egos of the pride, the insulters.
The deserving, he might say.
The "He-needed-killin'" defense
of the time. Of course, the notches
on the gun were just talk. "Notches can
snag your hand when you draw," he said.
But after a few years, the avengers come,
and then the neck never stops turning.

The brothers and fathers and uncles
of the foolish would ride the miles
to stand before him, call him a murderer,
which he didn't like, and draw. And die.
After a while, the face-to-face challenges
stopped, and they began to bushwhack
and backshoot, anything to get the drop
on the bastard—and they died too.
Most of them.

In Deadwood, at the end,
glaucoma slowly taking the eyes
that once could drill a hole
in a silver dollar at fifty yards,
the newly married cardplayer,
immortality assured, died
holding an excellent hand,
shot in the back by one
whose fame would be shorter.

Was it really five men,
Mr. Hickok, sir? Five at once?
Wow.

Autumn 2003 – Winter 2004
Sunland, Ca.

Chinese Humour

A father and a boy were walking
down the street together...

Laughter has no aim.
It's just scattershot detonation,
a sound from thought collisions,
a yelp, like sudden pain.
Each tribe learned to make fun
of other tribes to pass the time
when they weren't killing them.

And the boy was making faces
at the father...

And, though language changed
with each border, costume with climate,
there were certain legends -- the flood,
the messiah, the spirit-animal -- that spread
to all corners, and took hold.

And the father said, "Boy, if you continue
to make faces, you will turn into a monster."

Jokes, too, traveled these vast
tracts, multiplied like subspecies, found
niches in the collective consciousness.
There were those who told them
and those who could not. There was
a hierarchy.

And the boy said to the father, "Father, you must have made many faces when you were a boy."

And so, in each place, the stories were told differently. Just a bit differently.

You see, the father was a monster in the eyes of the boy.

16 May 2003 – Caribbean Sea

EXCUSES

The bone must go, the wish can stay.
The kiss don't know what the lips will say.

Tom Waits

Excuses

I could say she was beautiful,
and appeared available. Her desire
striding to me like a priest in
procession; confident,
prepared to speak only
in profundities.

Excuses are such pure things.
I could say I needed it, but
I wanted it says it better.

A psychiatric pony,
trained to whirl and whinny
for sugar-lumps, sleeping
on straw-piles, waiting for
something that comes, and
something that never comes.

I could say that my mother
didn't breast-feed me. It
wasn't encouraged then.

I love you has become
one word, like hello,
or sorry, or when? I no longer
gallop home expectant.
I think of my breath
when we kiss.

My premature brother came
crying for food when I was not
yet eighteen months old.

I could say they stopped
touching me, and this is
no one's fault. It has given
me everything I use, waiting
for something that comes,
and something that never comes.

22 – 26 April 2004   Caribbean Sea

Artery

This is my heart, this footsore
thing, awash in blood, blockage,
and uncertainty. It makes
no murmur, even the strange
speech howled in sleep.

When I dream of my father,
I awaken and rush to phone him,
anxious to know whether he has flown
off to my unconscious forever.

When I dream of a woman,
I awaken with the fervent hope
that her name was not among
my night-cries. Sometimes I stare
at the woman who says she loves me,
looking for clues.

It's in the needle,
the blood on the sleeve.
This is my heart, shrouded in all this
laughter, running from everything.

16 May, 2003 – Caribbean Sea

Like Words

Perhaps it was something you said
about happiness and its inevitable partner.
The sound of your voice, like salt water
on stone, the delicious conversation
underpinning desire, and the fervent, almost-
honest bursts of possibility. The easy way
our arms roped and separated, meaning
nothing at all or nothing very much.

How we both watched when the other
wasn't aware, seeing secret things
we may never tell or even have the need
to recall, that closed the distances,
allowed the talk penetrable openings.
And what you said about happiness and hard
endings stays with me, like words
floating in a small room.

18 – 20 April 2004
Caribbean Sea

Previously Unknown Fact

She says
that failure
to say what
is true, a sin
of omission,
is a lie.

So,
add this.
Everything
I have
never said
is untrue.

December – 2002

Cheater

Once she caught me cheating
at Scrabble.

It was embarrassing.

She was concentrating so hard
on her own letters,
I thought she'd miss it.

Then, reaching
for the space, a perfect
word in her fingers,
she stopped.

'Infidel has only one L,'
she said.

Spring 2002

Four Wish-Meditations

I

It is not as you think,
this way of mine, this
sadness. (The television
next door is quite loud as
I write this. The old man
living there is as deaf as
I will one day be.)

If I cannot sleep it keeps you up.
If I cannot love it worries
no one. I have loved, after all.

I will run away
again, (slower this time) and this
brings a smile, for no one
I once gleefully imagined
would miss me,
would miss me.

II

I wish I could tell you
my loud thoughts. (Have
you ever pushed a full
minute of thought into one
screaming second? I have.)

How empty I feel, how un-
muscular. How I wanted you
to see me a certain way; an
admiration, I suppose,
a blood-lust.

 How I wished you would stop
working because you were shaky
with need of me, like food.
Your eyes blurring, your sweet
legs unsure. And in my arms
complex calories would be found.

You often say, "Well, you didn't
grow up in my family." But
of course, I did.

III

I need to hear what I don't know,
love what I cannot see,
breast-blinded, pressed
between pages.

What you need is too easy.
No thought is required to trim
and cut, wash and fold.
I pick up after myself as habit now.

I would so rather
worship your white skin,
get on my knees and drink you
as though I just stumbled in
from a desert.

IV

I could tell you why
I don't want to have another
long talk in darkness,
about our felonies
and disinclinations.

The kind where sleep comes
after as a great peace
because ideas have been floated
and found not as dangerous
on the open air as they seemed
in the mind.

Because then
I will think this again, that
we have spoken and not died
of shame, and nothing
really changed, did it?

10 June, 2003
Sunland, Ca.

Deep Down

First she said she couldn't take
year-round sports on TV. So he
dropped football from his watch calendar.

Then she said he should stop spending money
so freely. He worked very hard on that.

Then she wondered if she'd have to leave him
because of the drugs, and he must have sensed it
because he quit cold turkey and managed to stay off.

Then she said he shouldn't take her lack of lust
personally. He should work on his anger.

Service, she said, not gifts.
Service was what she needed.
Not flattery, not affection, provisions, respect, mad
passionate love poems, no. Someone to empty
the dishwasher, clean up, pick up, fold, put away,
and stop watching so damn much TV.

But he still watches a lot of TV,
because, deep down, he's always been a rebel.

September 9 – 15 2001
NY – Bermuda

Untold

She says, 'You don't think
I love you.' And I let it pass,
the point of even friendly
argument long past, lost.

Could I convince her I do
think she loves me? In her way,
I mean. Would qualifying it
spoil the fun?

I prepare a silent defense,
eyes closed through a long flight
alone to somewhere. I look up
the word 'love' in the OED.

Of course she loves me.
The daisy test is a circle
of even numbers, a perfect
empty explanation.

'The profoundly tender or passionate
affection for a person of the opposite
sex.' Really? They should change that.
Not correct enough these days.

Or 'sexual passion or desire
or its gratification.' No. That's lust.
Maybe my threshold's too high.
Maybe she's right.

March 2004

Holds

There is anger, I suppose,
in both revel (me) and repression (you).
A way of seeing things.

The world dying in a poisoned shudder,
the end of education,
crime and betrayal.

Our children, of course. One like me,
a sneaky pleaser. One like you, quiet,
thoughtful, made of iron.

A history of not getting
what we really want, which
we both tend like a cherished garden.

A house, our second,
which we speak of selling one day
as though it could actually happen.

Your secrets,
my lies,
lots of furniture.

Spring – Summer 2004

The Waters Off Labadee

Sometimes you can feel it –
feel it coming, the rest of your life.
(In the movies, they say, 'the rest of
your miserable life'.) The water is
a glassy grey-blue under the high sun.
I am the high son, firstborn male
with the attachment on my name.
The wanted one – it's almost funny –
able to lord it over the second
and third sons so easily. Not true,
of course. Some are born to lead
and others just born in the lead.

I whisper nothings to her skin,
wondering if there's any way back.
She thinks she knows what I do not know.
It is the weakness I love most in her.
She is also a firstborn, though certainly
more comfortable with the implications,
the duties. She will never walk naked
through the yard just to see how it feels.

Occasionally, there is a moment of not
knowing where you are – suspended
between knowledge-states. Wide awake
but not traveling anywhere

Toward shore the water turns khaki,
reflecting the hills. Sky and land
are pure colours, water always the mix.
Sometimes you just have to say something, even
though you know that once the words strike
the air, they will never be yours again.

Oct 22 – 31 2003
Haiti – Jamaica – Miami – Boise – Reno – Los Angeles

Thinking

I think of kissing you,
leaning against brick,
under a rainswept awning,
your gloved hand pressing
my shoulder.

There is a seeking in us,
an itch for passion-proving
scars, a fear of letting
anything go, because then
it would all go.

I think of kissing you,
somewhere cold and damp,
tasting blood.

Spring 2004
Sunland, Ca.

EXCUSES

SHIPS

Divide the waters from the land,
If daring ships, and men profane,
Invade the inviolable main;
The eternal fences overleap,
And pass at will the boundless deep.

Horace

Ships

For Don Coles

Don is telling a story
about meeting Sylvia Plath
at a party in England, mid fifties.

He wasn't impressed, he says,
because she was American,
and he'd met American girls before.

He wanted to meet some exotic
British girls who, rumour had it,
liked everything.

If she had intrigued you, I think,
it could have been, 'Don, Don,
you bastard, I'm through.'

But I don't say it. Instead I mention
that I have a recording of her reading
'Daddy', and listening to it makes me cry.

He shrugs, as thought the hi-how-are-you
meeting was nothing special, although
he remembers it.

He doesn't say if he found any exotic
British birds. Or that Sylvia moved on,
met another poet, never grew old.

January – April 2002

Orion

At night on my porch,
searching the sky over
the giant twin pines,
my brother's long head
turning this way and that.
"There's the Dipper," he said,
and I saw it and understood
the name for the first time.

My star was not visible.
Odd, since it always seems
to be over the garage, my garage.
There for me most nights to imagine
steering along its way to Tahiti
or some such place. I told my brother
of the sea people who navigate
by stars alone. Stars they have named.

The tiny thrush who nests above
my door flew in and out. A coyote
ghosted by, the dogs in uproar
at the scent of a free life. We spoke
of everything but age and love, strangely
unafraid of each other. Perhaps
for the first time.

April 2003
Sunland, Ca.

Mountain Water

Watching my daughters swim
in that most alluring tourist attraction,
the pool; its sun-kaleidoscopic waters
rippled in turquoise, their favorite
artificial color.

This morning, we walked
Andreas Canyon, along the famous
fault line trail, giant rusty shield-rocks
swooping above like deities,
the worshippers long dead.

Thousand-year-old palms
that sprouted after the ice age quake
that rumbled this perfect valley
stood hardy, and somewhere below us,
water, that most enabling sound.

Mountain water, cool under
the palm canopy, rushing, tumbling
over the stone descents. Virgin
snow-water, here where rain is extinct,
a creek that believes it's a river.

My daughters called in fear
when I stepped out into the flow,
balancing my suddenly-young self
on smooth wet rocks, frightening
toads and jubilant mosquitoes.

Now I watch in fear as they dogpaddle
through the chlorine world they adore.
And, sunblocked and fossiled
in my chair, I call out Jesus be careful,
mindful of sea monsters.

18 – 24 April 2003. Palm Springs – Los Angeles

Little Sister

Nine years between us long fallen
away, and often I think of you
in your studio, the perfect cold
of Toronto most months, the photos
of wonderful places hanging around,
the bookcase full of opera scores,
the small piano gleaming black.
There is a safety in imagining you there;
teaching, singing, brushing your hair.

And we have a strange love, unlike
the normal cottages of growing up
under one roof, the same parents, though
at different times. The love we have
expressed so perfectly in secrets shared
and helpless, nude laughter. We are
what we have always wanted, at once
cocksure in knowing what no one else knows.
Adoring each moment, each pose.

And now you are leaving, as I did.
Leaving our country and going off where
you can't be visited too often, and you'll
have to learn new things. Become the toast
of some new civilization. How I will miss
not knowing the colour of your bedroom,
the streets you will stride so confidently,
the new city you will see and absorb alone.
A place too expensive to fly to, or phone.

Today I painted the front window frames
of the new house you haven't seen,
and the colour was wrong. It will have to be
redone. And, maneuvering the ladder in and out
of rosebushes, cursing the thorns, I thought
only of you, learning an old language,
 boxing up the heavy things that cannot go
with sadness, yet eager. I remember then.
Making plans to escape and be new again.

8--9 May 2003, Sunland, Ca.

The News

A newspaper, my first in days,
crackles in my dry hands. My new
bifocals seek out information
with a suddenly recognized hunger.

Sitting on the floor, watching my father
read the evening paper. I am three, perhaps four.
I know he's reading but the words seem infinite
up there above his crossed-mountain legs, thick
Irish hands snapping the pages in rhythm.

A woman has drowned her children
in the bath, and then burned the house down.
Several interesting movies are coming out.
The government is full of shit.

I delivered papers, a lost city to a boy or girl
today. They would dump fifty papers
on the curb and I would fold them, stuff them
in the giant sling-bag, and ride off, hands blackened.
The year of the October Crisis, and the woman who
had nine babies at once and they all died.

I cover the sports, wins and losses, laugh
and swear at the editorials, soaking it all up,
squeezing each page like a dying sponge.
Between the lines it's always raining.

The first woman I ever saw naked
was on that paper route. First live woman.
There was a magazine somebody found that
showed us a few new things that winter.
It was the first time I ever heard the word succulent,
knowing exactly what it must mean.

The waitress picks up my thumb-crumpled paper,
notices me writing, and in a heavily
Slavic voice, asks, "Is it just come to you,
or do you have to think about it?"
Yes.

23 June 2004

A Slight Pause

I tried to call you
on your birthday last year.
The day before your child
turned one. My mother had sent
the birth notice a year earlier.
It may have been your fortieth.
I remember thinking that, and wanting
to hear your happiness, let it
enter my veins again, long after
everything happened.

But no operator could locate
the seven digits that would produce you.
I spoke to some old friends who had
lost touch with you, though I heard
no regret at this occurrence. One of them,
an ex-boyfriend of yours before me,
now divorced, said he was newly, hopelessly
in love with a much younger woman. "There
will now be a slight pause," I said, "While
a sheet of envy settles over me."

I remembered the night you told me
you had decided to date me exclusively.
I remembered you rising early
and stealing from my bed to move
your car, lest it be ticketed, returning
to rouse me for your pleasure;
your reassuring fingers in my hair.

Had we spoken, I doubt I would have
written this. I would have hung up
and thought of much more to say.

10 February, 2003
Sunland, Ca.

Beckie

Dinner with a girl from the old, old street,
four years my senior. Our sisters were friends.
We rhyme off the names that filled each house,
amazed that they reside with us yet, waiting
to be called. I mention the trombone-playing
girl I loved at fourteen, and she promises to find
her for me. I tell her of my decades-old fantasy
that I'll finish a show in Somewhere (Sask.) and my
trombone-playing girl will appear, sly smile and all.
I don't mention that I've scoured phonebooks from
Charlottetown to Prince Rupert for her, knowing she
must be married now, surely a mother, and certainly
not listed under her perfect adolescent name.

The girl from the old, old street, who seems to exist
in a smile-warp, has never married. The Calgary night
has grown colder as we exit the eatery. Three hooded
young men stare at us as we start across the lot. She
takes my hand as if it's the most natural thing,
and we walk home from school.

December – 2002

Unsent Letter

Dear Myshkin, I saw you,
working in the fancy restaurant.
I stood there and stared at you
for close to a minute, or three years.
You were shucking oysters.
I saw your white cap and long sleeves,
moving as a musician's do, your hard
brown eyes firing their sparks.
I hoped you would feel me there,
and turn your momentarily unstudied gaze
to find me, then I was afraid you would, so
I left. I knew it would spoil everything –
your happiness, our perfect incommunicado
relationship, the charm of your adopted city –
if I called your name. The full name
you anxiously insist upon or the nickname
you hate. You said you'd put me in
the hospital if I appeared, so I disappeared.
But I saw you. From enough of a distance
I think. Later you would tell people
I was stalking you.

The hell with it. Start again.

Dear Myshkin,
you look thin.

7 January, 2003
Key West

John Wing jr. ● 61

A Series of Short Poems About my Dick

I

Measured it once, oh
twelve or thirteen
years old, I guess.
But the ruler
was only six
inches long,
and I've grown
since then.

II

The doctor was
Scottish, (lucky me)
and gave me what
is called a 'Dorsal Split'.
So I am circumcised
and I have foreskin.
It's not really
so bad, except that
all my life I've had
an unnatural fear
of kilts.

III

When she dunked me
in the river, mother
must have held me
by the cock and balls.
Must have seemed big then
because I was so small.
I no doubt cried until
long after I was dry,
and no one ever told me
it would be my weakest point.

IV

In high school,
in the locker room
one day, a friend
said mine was too
big. Women wouldn't
like it. Oddly enough,
I wasn't concerned.

V

Once, at the end
of an LSD trip,
I went looking for it
in a washroom.
Devoid of moisture
from the 12-hour stone,
it had inverted,
and did not appear
until the next day,
whereupon I immediately
masturbated, for
diagnostic reasons
as much as exercise.

VI

Eventually,
I named it 'Bob'.
No particular reason.
I may have thought
'Robert' was too formal.

Aug 7-8, 2002
Cayman Islands

Watch Me

I never looked around my little city enough
to find it in my head. Knew only the small wisps,
the names of streets, but not the names of trees,
the taste of air around the foundry, but not
the taste of character and place and time.
I recall enjoying the acrid swallows of oxygen
while delivering papers on my first bike,
the soft grass of the parish hall lawn where
we played football, the absence of dogs.

But I didn't watch things. Didn't see the only divorced
woman on our street, although I played with her son.
Rode in a hundred cars without ever noting how you
drive one. Had no understanding of those who lived
in our house. Brothers, sisters, parents – all existing
on my vexed plain as obstacles, things to hide from.
I read the wrong books, failed all the table-tests,
became defiant, angry me because I wanted to
be like them – the good son, the honourable
daughter, the talented one.

I can feel loved by applause or provoked laughter,
hold a grudge in my fist until it's wet, write poems
about writing poems in a choirloft, or anger-jokes.

Once, in acting class, we did an exercise where you had to count to ten using an emotion, the emotion growing stronger with each number. I chose anger, being a coward. I had reached four when the teacher stopped me. "You can't go six places higher than that with your anger," she said.

Autumn – 2002

No History

I have discovered all I want
is nothing very much. A bicycle
and young legs to ride it. Failing
that, I suppose it might be fun
to go back and live some odours
again, with no history. No
history at all.

Hot rain on hot leaves. Big, glass-
filling drops. Straight, windless,
summer-perfection rain falling on
the great tree that fell across Brock
street that Friday. So we had three
dangling days until the city came
and chopped up the whole idea.

The hair of a girl, whose name I still
recall easily after thirty years, at an early
dance. It had been washed that afternoon,
and was slightly perspired from the b-ball
court dance-floor activity. Impossibly
straight, silver-brown. And music, and hands,
feet finding purchase on water.

I have told the tale of the lightning bolt
hitting the street in front of my bike
several times. My daughters never tire
of such things, bless them. The desperate
ride through the sudden storm, fresh
paperback in one pocket, and no history.
None at all.

Winter 2003-2004

Flashing Before

In the very last light,
under a favoured blanket, perhaps,
will I remember the sand
in my father's bed, the way
his belt buckle lay on the floor
and then traveled upward, always
at the same speed?

Shaving together,
his Burma-shave brush dipping wetly
into the wooden lather-bowl.

Or will it be my sister, behind
our house that summer night,
crying softly as she fell again and again,
trying to ride the blue two-wheeler,
training wheels removed.
My father's voice calling,
"Do it again," after each crash.

Or will they all come in a rush,
as though someone called fire.
Nothing sticking, just the flood-flash
of images tumbling everywhere.

Richard dangling over the alligator pit,
Dad chasing Tony to the water's edge,
the dead football player at Tiger stadium,
and girls, barenaked girls.

It may come as an impossible bursting
after a long wait, the way orgasm takes
forever until it's done. A flood to
a trickle. Who really cares?

December – 2002

Not Writing

When you saw me,
it may have looked like
I was writing. Head bent
to the blue-scratched page,
hair in the light.

But I was smelling an old shoe,
crawling through a closet.
A large-voiced man had his hands
on me. And the shoe was huge.
My whole arm disappeared into it.

I was watching someone drive away,
screaming back words at me. Standing
on an empty, day-lit Toronto street,
not feeling tall or even real, as her anger
carpeted the widening space between us.
Just another ending.

Nobody ever came in those days,
wondering why I wasn't in bed.
I never avoided anyone's bed
just to write, either.

But no matter what you thought
you saw, it wasn't me. I was long gone.
A new city, or (most likely)
an old one, pinwheeling from one color
to the next, unaware (perfection of choice!)
of almost everything.

'Come to bed '. As though you
can walk away in middle age
from the fields, the thighs,
the mouths filled with words,
the crimes that turned into money-
making anecdotes, the infrequent truth,
the wet paper melting in your hands.

I won't answer. I won't say, 'Soon,'
or, 'I'm working.' You started talking then
and you may have thought I was writing.
Unrecorded images zapping through me
like a bad trailer. Then you touched me,
and my scream may have frightened you,
my arm sleeved in a giant's shoe, the judge-voice
calling. Not frightened, no. Just amazed.
Up late alone, discussing the past with
a leaded window. Not writing. Just
trying to clean the blood off my life.

7 February, 2003
Houston to Los Angeles

The Rink

Coming into a room, I smell cake
& ice cream. Through a long window,
I see the rink. A little girl's birthday
skating party has just ended, and the
breathless high frequency of presents
has begun. Standing by my wife
and the birthday girl's Mom, I realize
with some anger that we'll be here
for another hour at least. I've come
too early. Glancing out the window,
I see a hockey game has begun.

Cold in here. My dress shirt
that's too warm outside isn't enough.
I shiver to the glass, alone on this
side. The seats are over there, semi-
filled – parents, etc. A professional
set up. Boards, glass, good ice,
electronic scoreboard, benches, penalty
box, red goalposts. And that smell
I've never attempted to identify but
always known. Cold sweat and wool,
perhaps? A young hockey smell.

I see my thirty-odd year absence
has not changed the game. Still
skates & sticks, shin pads under
leggings wrapped with tape, (we used
industrial rubber bands) suspender
pants, shoulder pads, jersey, helmet
& gloves. I see surnames stitched above
numbers on each player's back. Don't think
we had that. My last pair of gloves, huge
steel-thumbed beauties, cost $17. A sum
my father said was 'criminal'.

White shirts against blue shirts
in furious chase. Most of the action
in the so-called neutral zone. I wonder
what we called it? Almost every pass
is intercepted. The theory seems to be: skate
with the puck until you lose it, then fall
back into whatever position you recall,
and wait for fate to bring the puck back.
(I realize I later used this theory in relationships)
Breakaway, that most perfect word to describe
that occasionally most perfect thing. Glove save.

God I want to jump out there and play.
I'm much bigger now, and I really
understand the positioning and flow
of the game. Then I had no idea.
I look for that one player who gets it.
There always seemed to be one in our league.
Skate rings around everyone, handle the puck,
score. Years later, you'd see him working in coveralls in
a print shop, no bigger than he was at eleven, never to
leave town. There doesn't seem to be a dominator in
this group.

By the time my wife & daughter
come looking for me, I'm yodeling advice
& encouragement, wrapped tight , warmed
by the speed. That's why I want to play. I know
how to pay attention now. As a young, goalless
player, I would come to the bench after a shift
and chat with my linemates. Suddenly my
father's tympanic voice would find me,
("Watch the GAME!") snapping my head back
to the action. My daughter tugs at my shirt, but
I can't leave. I know everything now.

February – March – April 2004

Directions

North of Sarnia,
take the third concession road
and when you see the grain silo
that says Rokeby, stop and look
all around. There's no sign, but
many people believe that's
the exact middle of nowhere.

If a head appears,
cradle it, one hand
underneath and one
to the side. Don't pull,
let it come out by itself.
Once the first shoulder
comes, the whole body
shoots out very quickly.
Be careful.
Be ready.

Insert shelf into groove,
put in pegs to secure & realize
the rough edge means you've
put them all in backwards.
Consider, for a moment or two,
leaving it like this, try to convince
yourself she won't notice, then
take shelf apart with special screw-
driver (provided) or axe.

Don't worry about the camera.
Don't think about the camera.
The camera does not exist.

Take the San Diego Freeway to
the Ronald Reagan Freeway to
the Foothill Freeway to
the Glendale Freeway to
the Golden State Freeway to
the San Bernardino Freeway to
the Slauson Cut-Off. Get out
your car, cut off your Slauson, get
back in your car.

Ask if you can remove her shirt.
If she says yes, unbutton it from behind
and slide it off as slowly as you're able.
Ask if you can kiss her neck and shoulders.
If she says yes, kiss the neck first and move
toward the shoulder taking note of any
sound she makes that could be pleasure.
Ask if you can take her bra off. If she says
yes, grasp both sides of the back strap
with thumb and forefinger. Pull the right
side and push the left side simultaneously,
not too hard. It should come apart easily.
Then slowly guide the shoulder straps down
the arms. Turn her toward you and try not
to gasp when you see them. When you kiss her
on the lips, after asking and if she says yes,
wait for her tongue to materialize before
inserting your own. Practice, practice, practice.
Imagine this scenario again and again, repeating
to yourself, If she says yes, if she says yes.

If she says no
at any point, stop
immediately, put
your pants back on
and turn up the TV.

The curb is for the loading
and unloading of passengers
only. No Parking.
Unattended vehicles will
be subject to immediate
tow-away. Do not
leave your car unattended.

Brush up-and-down,
not side-to-side.

If a foot appears,
gently push it back in
and massage the belly
to try and turn the child
around. If this fails and
the foot appears again,
wait for the second foot,
and try to guide it out
as gently as possible.
Watch that the umbilical cord
doesn't get tangled
around the neck.
Don't panic.

If a hand appears,
call your doctor.

Take the first left and
the second right.
You can't miss it.

(Yes, I can)

Write several funny jokes,
figure out the sequence
in which they work best ,
go onstage and repeat
them until somebody laughs,
then get paid.

Lather, rinse, repeat.

Go home the regular way
if you're alone, and the short
way if you're being chased.
Know the difference
in the short way between
winter and summer. The short way
is much shorter if you run.

Take the River road
until it ends.
Dive.

Don't drink the water.
Don't fly off the handle.
Don't wear white after Labour Day.
Don't take the name of the Lord in vain.
Don't steal, kill, or lie,
unless absolutely necessary.
Don't make me come over there.

Love you neighbour
as yourself, up to
but not including
mutual masturbation.

Wear a condom.
It may rain.

Never volunteer.
Never go in until at least
an hour after you've eaten.
Never say never.

Go down High,
up Elm, and over Bridge,
and keep driving
past the Esso station
and the KFC until you see
a sign that says ARROW.
Ignore that and keep going,
bearing left as the road
curves right, go about a mile
or five/eighths of a mile till you see
the old barn with the ad on it,
then past the church that
burned down last year
and you're right there.

Fall 2004. Sunland, Ca.

Acknowledgements

Some of these poems (okay, two) were published in
ARC and the anthology, *Body Language*, edited by
John B. Lee.

Thanks to Howard Aster and everyone at Mosaic Press.
Book number four. So far. So good.

Thanks to Marty and Donna Gervais, Windsor's Festival of
the Book, & The Book Keeper in Sarnia.

Special thanks to Don Coles, who not only befriended
me but also gave his critique of the manuscript in, shall
we say, its intermediate stage. His copious notes and
astounding critical acumen made me blush and made
this a much better book. I am greatly indebted to him.

I'm not sure they had anything to do with this book, but
apparently if you don't thank the Canada Council they
get really pissed off. So, thanks.